W9-CQV-873

ODELL
BECKHAM JR.

BY PAUL BOWKER

SportsZone

An Imprint of Abdo Publishing
abdopublishing.com

abdopublishing.com

Published by Abdo Publishing, a division of ABDO, PO Box 398166, Minneapolis, Minnesota 55439. Copyright © 2018 by Abdo Consulting Group, Inc. International copyrights reserved in all countries. No part of this book may be reproduced in any form without written permission from the publisher. SportsZone™ is a trademark and logo of Abdo Publishing.

Printed in the United States of America, North Mankato, Minnesota
042017
092017

THIS BOOK CONTAINS
RECYCLED MATERIALS

Cover Photo: Al Tielemans/AP Images
Interior Photos: Al Tielemans/AP Images, 1; Kathy Willens/AP Images, 4–5; John Albright/ Icon Sportswire, 7; Tony Gutierrez/AP Images, 9; Gerald Herbert/AP Images, 10–11, 12; Seth Wenig/AP Images, 14–15; Aaron M. Sprecher/AP Images, 17; Julio Cortez/ AP Images, 18–19, 23; Matt Rourke/AP Images, 21; Doug Benc/AP Images, 24–25; Evan Pinkus/AP Images, 27, 29

Editor: Todd Kortemeier
Series Designer: Craig Hinton

Library of Congress Cataloging-in-Publication Data
Names: Bowker, Paul D., author.
Title: Odell Beckham Jr. : high flying receiver / by Paul D. Bowker.
Other titles: High flying receiver
Description: Minneapolis, MN : Abdo Publishing, 2018. | Series: Playmakers | Includes bibliographical references and index.
Identifiers: LCCN 2016962128 | ISBN 9781532111471 (lib. bdg.) | ISBN 9781680789324 (ebook)
Subjects: LCSH: Beckham, Odell, Jr., 1992- --Juvenile literature. | Football players--United States--Biography--Juvenile literature.
Classification: DDC 796.332 [B]--dc23
LC record available at http://lccn.loc.gov/2016962128

TABLE OF CONTENTS

Odell Beckham Jr.

CHAPTER 1

THE BIG EASY

O dell Beckham Jr. was running toward the end zone. It was his first year in the National Football League (NFL). He was a rookie wide receiver for the 2014 New York Giants. They were playing the rival Dallas Cowboys on Sunday Night Football.

Quarterback Eli Manning threw his way. The pass looked high. Beckham stretched his right arm up.

Odell Beckham Jr., *right*, **makes an incredible one-handed catch on November 23, 2014.**

Beckham somehow came down with the ball. It was a miracle touchdown. That one play turned him into an immediate star for the Giants. Video of the play became popular around the world. It was named Play of the Year at the 4th Annual NFL Honors.

It was a play Beckham may have dreamed about as a child.

Beckham wasn't the only NFL star to attend Isidore Newman School. His future Giants teammate and quarterback Eli Manning also went there. So did Eli's brothers, Cooper and Peyton.

He grew up in New Orleans. The city is known in the Deep South as "the Big Easy." Both of Odell's parents played sports at Louisiana State University (LSU). His mother, Heather, ran track. Odell Beckham Sr. played football. They both taught Odell what it would take to succeed as an athlete.

Odell tried lots of sports. He played football, baseball, basketball, and soccer. From age nine through 12, he played on a traveling baseball team. He played center field and was a

Beckham made the 2011 US Army All-American Bowl as one of the country's best high school football players.

leadoff hitter. He played forward for a traveling soccer team. He was also a talented point guard in basketball.

Football soon took over. Odell went to high school at the Isidore Newman School. He played both football and basketball. One of the honors of his senior year was playing in the US Army All-American Bowl.

Odell made his own football history at Newman. He caught 50 passes for 1,010 yards in his senior season. Only one other receiver in Newman history had reached 1,000 yards in one season.

Beckham had many scholarship offers. Some were from the best college football programs in the country. Mississippi State, Nebraska, and Ole Miss all wanted him. His final choice was between LSU and the University of Miami.

Odell caught 19 touchdown passes that year. He also ran for 331 yards and six touchdowns. He passed for another touchdown. He returned two punts for touchdowns. He also played on defense and had four interceptions.

Odell's success in high school led him to a top college. Many offered him scholarships. He chose to follow in the footsteps of his parents. He became an LSU Tiger.

Beckham catches one of two passes in his first college game against the University of Oregon.

Odell caught 41 passes for 475 yards in his freshman season. He scored two touchdowns.

One of his big moments was a 51-yard touchdown against the Kentucky Wildcats. He caught the pass. He broke a tackle. Then he faked out several defenders. He got free and ran in for the score. Odell was on his way to becoming one of the best players in LSU history.

Odell Beckham Jr.

CHAPTER 2

TIGER LEGEND

Odell Beckham Jr. will always remember his 19th birthday.

It was November 5, 2011. He was a freshman at LSU. Beckham and the top-ranked Tigers were in Tuscaloosa, Alabama. They played the second-ranked Alabama Crimson Tide.

Beckham later called it one of the most exciting games he ever played in. He compared it to a Monday Night Football game in the NFL.

Beckham, *33*, celebrates a touchdown catch with teammate Jarvis Landry in 2011.

Beckham, *3*, gets congratulations from teammates after scoring a touchdown in a 2013 game.

Beckham caught two passes. LSU won 9–6 in overtime. But most importantly, the Tigers silenced the Alabama crowd of more than 100,000 screaming Tide fans.

That game was one highlight in a season of many. Beckham and the Tigers won 13 games. They played for the national championship. It was a rematch with Alabama. This time the Crimson Tide came out on top. It was LSU's only loss of the season.

Beckham became an offensive machine in his next two years at LSU. He started 12 games as a sophomore. He led the team with 713 receiving yards. And Beckham was not just a receiver. He also returned kicks. He led the Southeastern Conference (SEC) in punt returns his sophomore year. Two went for touchdowns.

It is all about the number three for Beckham. He began his college career at LSU wearing jersey No. 33. He switched to No. 3 in his junior season.

Beckham became one of the best offensive players in LSU history. His 4,118 total yards were the fifth most ever. His 143 catches ranked ninth. His 2,340 receiving yards were seventh. And Beckham played just three seasons. Many of the players ahead of him had played four.

After his junior year, Beckham chose to turn pro. He declared that he would enter the NFL Draft. A whole new career was set to begin.

Odell Beckham Jr.

GOING PRO

O dell Beckham Jr. stood as the national anthem played. His eyes became watery. Tears formed on his cheeks. But he wasn't sad. They were tears of joy. Beckham was about to play in his first NFL game for the New York Giants.

It was a long road to get there. Beckham was chosen in the first round of the 2014 NFL Draft in May. But he injured his hamstring just before training camp. Although he recovered, he hurt himself again.

Beckham catches his first NFL touchdown pass in his first career game.

Beckham was chosen with the 12th overall pick in the draft. Four other receivers were taken in the first round. But Beckham was the only one to make the Pro Bowl that season.

Beckham was finally healthy by the fifth game. And that is why he showed tears of joy. Beckham had a great first start. He had four catches for 44 yards. One went for a touchdown. The Giants beat the Atlanta Falcons 30–20. The crowd at Giants Stadium rose to applaud their new star.

His teammates and coaches were impressed. Giants coach Tom Coughlin stopped by his locker after the game. He gave Beckham some encouraging words. He told him there were many more games like this to come.

Beckham was the Giants' top draft pick, so fans expected a lot. When he got hurt, they wondered if he'd ever live up to the hype. Playing well in his first game proved that he'd earned his place on the team.

Beckham celebrates a first down in a 2014 game against the Indianapolis Colts.

Odell Beckham Jr.

CHAPTER 4

ONE-HANDED WONDER

O dell Beckham Jr. was healthy for the rest of the 2014 season. He had his first two-touchdown game two weeks later. The next week, he exploded. He caught eight passes for 156 yards. Beckham's numbers were impressive. But the highlight of 2014 was still to come. His catch against the Dallas Cowboys quickly became an unforgettable play.

Quarterback Eli Manning, *right*, congratulates Beckham on his one-handed touchdown grab against Dallas.

Video clips of the miracle one-handed touchdown grab were everywhere. Back home, Beckham's sister, Jasmine, watched the play on television. She screamed and ran down the stairs of their Louisiana home.

That one play turned Beckham into a star. It became the type of catch he was known for. Kids tried to copy his one-handed grabs. They called it "Odelling." Video of the catch racked up millions of views on the internet. Broadcaster and former NFL receiver Cris Collinsworth said it was maybe the greatest catch he had ever seen.

Even National Basketball Association (NBA) star LeBron James tweeted about it. But the catch was no accident. Beckham practiced his one-handed grabs for years. His high school coach tried to get him to stop. But Beckham never had a drop. So he kept on doing it.

How does Beckham make those one-handed grabs? It's all in the fingers. He wears a triple-extra-large-size glove. His hands measured 10 inches (25.4 cm) long at the NFL Combine in 2014.

Beckham works on catching during pregame warmups.

Eli Manning saw Beckham practice those catches. LSU coach Les Miles saw the same thing while Beckham was in college.

A hint of what was to come came in an LSU game in 2013. Beckham was a kick returner for LSU. The Tigers were playing Georgia. The kickoff was sailing deep into the end zone. The ball looked like it was going over Beckham's head. He reached up and plucked it out of the air with one hand.

Beckham hoped the catch in 2014 was not his best. He wanted more of them. But most of all, he wanted to win. The Giants still lost that 2014 game against the Cowboys. And they finished 6–10 that season. Beckham wanted to change that.

Beckham's rookie season was remarkable. It was one of the best rookie seasons in New York Giants history. Beckham missed four games. But he still caught 91 passes for 1,305 yards. He scored 12 touchdowns. Both were records for a Giants rookie. He also was named 2014 Offensive Rookie of the Year. His play was even more impressive in his second season.

Beckham caught 96 passes in 2015. He started 15 games. He scored 13 touchdowns. His catches covered 1,450 yards. NFL records began to fall.

Beckham made NFL history on December 14, 2014. He had 12 catches for 143 yards and three touchdowns. He was the first rookie ever to have that many catches in one game.

Beckham comes down with a catch in a 2014 game, but an offensive penalty overturned the play.

Beckham made his 150th career catch in his 21st game. No other player had reached 150 catches so quickly. The previous record was 25 games. He tied the record for being the quickest to reach 2,000 career yards. It took him 21 games.

Odell Beckham Jr.

CHAPTER 5

MARCHING ON

One of Beckham's most memorable games came in 2015. The Giants played the Miami Dolphins. It was the first meeting in the NFL between Beckham and his LSU teammate Jarvis Landry. This was bigger than any catching competition they had in college.

The game was on national television on Monday Night Football. Landry had a big game with 11 catches for 99 yards.

Beckham was selected to the 2015 Pro Bowl following his outstanding rookie season.

Beckham was even better. He caught seven passes for 166 yards. Two of them were second-half touchdowns. The first tied it up. The second was the game winner. Beckham outran everybody for an 84-yard score. The Giants beat the Dolphins 31–24.

Beckham played his first NFL game in his hometown of New Orleans in 2015. The Giants played the New Orleans Saints in the Superdome. Beckham scored three touchdowns for the second time in his career.

Another record fell in the final game of 2015. Beckham finished with 187 career catches totaling 2,755 yards. No other NFL player had totaled that many yards in just two seasons. Randy Moss was the previous record holder. He had totaled 2,726 yards in his first two seasons. Beckham played in his second Pro Bowl after the season.

Off the field, Beckham started his own fashion line in 2016. He worked with New York designer David Helwani to produce a line of clothes. The collection made its debut in fall 2016.

Beckham makes another one-handed touchdown grab in a 2015 game against Washington.

It's called 13 x twenty after Beckham's jersey number and Helwani's company Twenty Tees. Beckham enjoys fashion and has attended several fashion shows.

Beckham's own fashion sense influenced the many tattoos that cover his arms. The tattoos began with a Sharpie pen. In high school, he would draw designs on his arms. He says each tattoo tells a story.

One thing was still missing in Beckham's career. He wanted to play in the playoffs. The Giants had losing records in his first two seasons.

Beckham met rapper Drake at a celebrity softball game in Houston. They became friends. Beckham has lived in Drake's house during the NFL offseason. He has appeared in videos dancing at Drake's home.

The Giants finally broke through in 2016. And Beckham turned in another great year. He had his third season with more than 1,300 receiving yards. In October, he racked up 222 yards against the Baltimore Ravens. That was a new career high. Beckham helped the Giants win 11 games. It was the most they had won since 2008. And it earned them a playoff spot.

Beckham got to make his first-ever playoff appearance. The Giants played the Green Bay Packers. The Giants had a 6–0 lead late into the first half. But the Packers got the lead back and didn't give it up. Beckham caught four passes for 28 yards.

Beckham gives his teammates a pep talk before the Giants'
2016 home opener.

The loss was a disappointment. But making the playoffs
was a step forward. Beckham has said his ultimate goal is to
win a Super Bowl. Giants fans believe that Beckham can take
them there.

FUN FACTS AND QUOTES

- Odell Beckham Jr. has a signed Tom Brady jersey. The two exchanged jerseys following an NFL preseason game in 2016. It is a common practice after professional soccer games. The Giants receiver and Patriots quarterback did it as a sign of respect.

- Beckham showed a lot of talent as a basketball player in his youth. "It was my first love," he said of the game.

- Shaquille O'Neal is a former NBA star who also played at LSU. Beckham calls him "Uncle Shaq." O'Neal became close friends with Odell Beckham Sr. while the two were at LSU. He is a family friend.

- Beckham and Jarvis Landry used to challenge each other to catching competitions when they played at LSU. The teammates used a football-passing machine to see who could make the most difficult catch. They used the machine so much that they broke it.

- Beckham spent his seventh-grade year in Washington, DC. His family had to move out of Louisiana for a year after Hurricane Katrina devastated New Orleans in 2005.

WEBSITES

To learn more about Playmakers, visit **abdobooklinks.com** These links are routinely monitored and updated to provide the most current information available.

GLOSSARY

All-American
Designation for players chosen as the best amateurs in the country in a particular sport.

conference
A group of schools that join together to create a league for their sports teams.

draft
The process by which teams select players who are new to the league.

freshman
A first-year student.

hamstring
A tendon located at the back of the upper leg.

offseason
The time of year when there are no games.

playoffs
A set of games played after the regular season that decides which team will be the champion.

Pro Bowl
The NFL's All-Star Game, in which the best players in the league compete.

rival
An opponent with whom a player or team has a fierce and ongoing competition.

rookie
A first-year player.

scholarship
Money given to a student to pay for education expenses.

sophomore
A second-year student.

tattoo
A permanent marking made on the skin.

INDEX

FURTHER RESOURCES

Cohen, Robert W. *The 50 Greatest Players in New York Giants Football History.* Lanham, MD: Rowman & Littlefield, 2014.

Frager, Ray. *LSU Tigers.* Minneapolis, MN: Abdo Publishing Company, 2013.

Schwartz, Paul. *Tales from the New York Giants Sideline.* New York: Sports Publishing, 2011.